WOMEN AT FORTY

Poems by

Sonia Gernes

UNIVERSITY OF NOTRE DAME PRESS
NOTRE DAME, INDIANA

Library of Congress Cataloging-in-Publication Data

Gernes, Sonia.
  Women at forty.

  1. Women—Poetry.   2. Middle aged women—Poetry.
I. Title.
PS3557.E685W66   1988   811'.54   87-40623
ISBN 0-268-01943-6 (pbk.)

. . . for Katherine Tillman and Mary Beth Blee

Contents

Acknowledgments

The author expresses gratitude to the Indiana Arts Commission, the Ragdale Foundation, the Fulbright Foundation, and the University of Notre Dame for their support at various points in the composition of these poems.

The author and publisher are grateful for permission to reprint the following poems which first appeared in these journals:

Beloit Poetry Journal: "Rites of Women."

The Georgia Review: "Women at Forty," "Family History," and "The Mushroom Eaters."

The Great Lakes Review: "The Ice Climbers."

The Great River Review: "The Picture Bride."

The Hiram Poetry Review: "Possum."

The Laurel Review: "Playing the Bells," "The Chinese Writers Visit Notre Dame," and "Freight."

Loblolly: "Eine Kleine Nachtmusik."

New Letters/University of Kansas City Review: "Waitomo: the River under the Earth," "Beneath Annie's Gown," and "The Many Kinds of Doubt."

Poetry Northwest: "First Notice," "Birds That Do Not Fly," "Letter to an Insomniac," and "Dust."

The Southern Review: "Little Sisters" and "What If a Woman."

Stanza: "Keeping the Hedge" and "This Lesson."

WOMEN AT FORTY

Women at forty wear their skin
like phases of the moon, like
crescents of pleasure bent to catch
all angles of light: the slippery
solstice, the fragile truce of noon.

Fresh from sleep, they are assured
that yesterday's paleness was but a sag
of light, an inconsequent fading.
Yet they wear their fullness conscious
of its snagged regrets, the lines
that web against the blooming.

Women at forty afford the dark side.
As the womb grows tighter,
they learn the shift in the lover's eye,
his taste for firmer flesh,
the secrets he is still avoiding:
again and again, they've kissed the skull
beneath the lover's grin, know
as surely as they know his thrust,
that what is full will soon be waning.

When sadness comes, women at forty
go without fear to a shuttered room,
bless themselves, bed down believing
that each effacement is but a rest,
a teasing dark before they ride again,
pushing the clouds from their right-of-way,
pulling the sea behind them.

1

. . . a woman who might be me

Then I bent above the cabbages,
the berries, acres of squash,
the pain of drawing water
three days past the birth. Sometimes

when I rise to light the fire,
I watch my husband sleep, a silt
of satisfaction covering his face.
I could never tell him

I am back at the rail, the ship
nudging a shaggy shore, my heart
a morsel I keep from gulls
who wheel and cry: *return, return* . . .

The darkness of my body is mine again,
and I close my eyes, sink
from the surface of the photograph,
from the moment I must open on the dock,
the fir trees, the lapping Sound,
the smiling men with photographs

—on that one still face
that will fix at the back of my eyes,
the image I must hold forever.

First Notice

The words are gone. It is that,
more than the other slippage—
the missing glasscase,
the iron left on—that troubles her.

Once, words were like a train,
an express that rumbled through her sleep,
a passenger line that was never late,
hurling across the borders
she needed to cross, bearing
her hopes, her quantity of luggage.

She is not really old; her brain
is too stable for that disease
which takes all names away,
but last night she could not think
what it was that held her eggs.
Kettle? Spider? Cast-iron box?
—a word as transient as the Zephyr
rolling out to Watertown, as the man
who left his brakeman's hat . . .

Sometimes she sees faces
blur like a window gathering speed,
finds photos of those vanished
from her Christmas card list.

Sometimes she dreams
she stands in a station
ready to board. The conductor
swings down the little stool-steps,
reaches to take the bag from her hand,
becomes—in a puff of steam—
something for which there is no name,
something that eyes her coldly, says:
Your ticket is expired, Ma'am;
this is not your destination.

ARTIFACTS

One lover left her a thimble,
another a stone. This one brings
a cut-glass plate, flowers so transparent
they might be mixed with rain.

She keeps such things in a cedar box:
old buttons, charms, notes that wash up
at the edges of life, a lockless key,
a leaf she found in a geography book.

She keeps them as solids, as ballast,
mornings when time floats away
—as thirty years before her father kept
rusty horseshoes, sleighbells in decay.

His sister left a single bed,
a hoard of stamps, a tiny sewing kit.
Stirring hankies in their lilac dust,
she wondered: can you make a life of this?

Now, when love is shaky, when the telephone
brings news of death from a fading house,
she hunts poems, pearls, the cut-
glass plate, the work she would want

remembered. Before the window
she fingers them: feather, shell,
a stalk of bittersweet—consoled by weight,
by stasis. When she is calm enough

she will think of things she did not save:

> an afternoon cottage by water
> a lift of curtains in the wind
> words that hover like a dragonfly
> in blue fluorescence
> his lips grown silent . . .
> the transparent, blue-etched wings.

BENEATH ANNIE'S GOWN

Anna Storcy
Hartford, Michigan
1823–1904

At first, it mattered little that she had no past.
Things washed up from the Civil War,
even in the North: a rifle butt,
a piece of uniform, a peg-legged
woman who could hold her own
at the cider mill, the blacksmith shop,
trading jokes in the gristmill crowd
until some clumsy neighbor brushed her skirts
and the sudden stillness round her mouth
became as dense as the grinding stone.

We were used to minor oddities.
We bought her flour, drank
cider from her press, ate the tartness
of her apple cakes at the Catholic Aid bazaar.
We made light of those who said
she was a fugitive, a pirate's moll, a murderess
with one leg tied up, skirts a clandestine cave
to which someone knew the route.
All of them were wrong.

The day she died, she sucked down silence
like water from a gourd,
the stone of her breath
harder than that other stone,

12

Francis Keasey's mortuary slab,
where eighty years of secrets all came clear:
the penis, the withered testicles,
the pale and flagging pendants of what she had denied.

Then we remembered everything:
the too-large hands, the furtive smile,
50-pound kegs tossed easily as onion sacks . . .
It might have been a gold-rush scheme, we said,
the plot to kill Lincoln, the psychopath
who chunked pieces of his wife
into the Finger Lakes, babies in the well . . .

But some of us were never sure.
We woke beside dreamers
whose distance was farther
than any night could go,
stood alone at a window of empty stars
and knew what we had always known:

beneath Annie's gown
was what we all possessed:
a spare and shrouded, unrepleted, still unfathomed
heart.

KEEPING THE HEDGE

*Remnants of original prairie are best
found along old fences and hedge-
rows—the narrow space a plow has
never touched . . .*
                    —May Thielgaard Watts

In October she will slip back to the prairie,
measuring light as she might measure
water in a glass. She will follow
the fencerows, the hedges, whispering names
of what has survived: cord grass, fleabane,
turkeyfoot, bluestem, wild rye . . .

Tossing car keys into waist-high grass,
she will run through cattail chimneys
adrift in their own smoky seeds, rock
in the wicker of the willows, recalling the spring
her first bloodroot stained a lap of shade.

She can never explain what men have called
"a distance" in her, what the children
have dug at with little pails and spades.
But the tracks of any tillage proclaim it:
what is once plowed under never comes back.

She thinks how she will wrap in the corduroy
of rubbing grasses, drape gentian rickrack
down her breast like a blouse. She will hold
herself steady under clouds of tenting nimbus.
She will keep her own hedge under sky like a sail.

14

EINE KLEINE NACHTMUSIK

Mozart and the memory elide tonight:
shadows, silvery as the leaves above her grave,
turn, tinkle that wind-music down
to the chilled green circle the headlights made.

Flowers shivered in their pots,
absorbed the icy rubbing of the leaves,
their undersides belly-white and brisk.

Why did you take me there
where I could not reach you,
my voice too flat for the night, the dark,
the dull hum of the motorcar?

The distant highway swished away all sound.
What light remained, hung in that tree,
that circle of cold. The shadows twisted
on your coat: tongues, tails,
small worried mammals of memory.

"Did you love her?" I wanted to say.
"And will I remember this?"
—in some other city, some other space,

watching a light catch leaves, catch
fragrance, catch the soundless sound
of your voice, the night, the motor humming,

the little music that we strained to hear,
and that one poised moment when I turned to go,
to step beyond the circle of the light?

This Lesson

*Each piece of writing has taught me
how to write it but was of no use for
the rest.* —Eudora Welty

I am back again in that forbidden house,
the stairway a backbone of oak, the rooms
awash with ancient light. "Look around,"
they say, and I peer into closets,
pull hats from shelves, lift out
corsets, cloaks—a freedom
they may not have intended.

The drawers are full of someone's past,
a sentence that begs to be finished.
I thrust both hands into drowsing silk,
a cocker spaniel barks
in another room, a bowl
is broken . . .

I search for parchment
(the oldest skin) in the rolltop desk,
find pencils instead, but something's wrong:
they are sealed, unsharpened, blunt
as a skull, a palisade of yellow staves
to warn me. Footsteps knock

against the staircase. I cannot move.
Voices come from nowhere, an argument
of sense with light. They call
another's name. "Go up," they say,
"to the attic . . ."

Possum

With blood down one side
and a tail thick enough
to whip the sap from trees,
he blots the morning sun
from my front walk,
turns a woeful snout
to look at me
then ambles like a drunk
across a dozen feet of lawn,
eyes focused on a country
that is either far or deep.

"Under the neighbor's porch,"
I say over the phone,
"hurt—or rabid—
looking for a place to hide, I think,"
but when the rescue van comes,
flashlights and poles assembled,
nothing stares back
from that shuttered womb;
nothing plays dead
in the earth-scented privacy,
the easeful dust
I thought that he was aimed for.

"I was sure he'd seek darkness,"
I say in defense,
but the woman points,
and there he is again,
claiming the lawn
in sunshine public as a courthouse square,

waiting while we move the cage,
then stepping up to the rubber noose,
offering his head . . .

Some wounds are like that.
They hound us out of the hiding place,
eat away the normal cloak
of decency,
leave us standing in sunlight,
with traffic going by,
leave us saying: Look, look!
Stop your cars!
This is real.
This is what happened.
I want you to believe this.
And I do not want to die.

PEOPLE WHO RUN AWAY

take things. You did not.
When the ladder left you
no foothold but grief,
you clawed the autumn air
but could not hold it,
cracked like a coconut
on patio cement. The doctors
glued you for hours
but every mirror showed the cracks.

After that, nothing you touched
was solid. Sums of the past
kept coming up different;
calendars disappeared.
The children grew faster than ever;
friends played hide and seek.

So this time you got it right.
You left us among the blank pages,
the missing checks, loaded
the last thing you could handle,
and aimed for the brightest nimbus,
triggered yourself to the eye of the cloud.

for J. D.

TAPS

The man against the fence is waiting for the gun.
He has been here since morning, a pale stump
in a line of old oak posts. It may go cheap,
he thinks—the bidding's slow, the field's
not shaded, the auctioneer's too old.

He gestures toward the graveyard down the road:
we'd all be there if the Krauts kept coming—
that's why he wants it—maximum deterrents
and safety in a shoulder load. He'd vote
to build more missiles any day. I tell him

I am waiting for a chest that locks, a safe,
a place to hold things—for birds whose song
will never fail the air. The auctioneer
keeps chanting; a small vase blooms, blue-veined
against the sky. Around us, shadows slip.

The bugled chant is waning: the day is going,
going . . . The notes are gone. We are standing
in a field that still exists. We are waiting
for the final bid, the last salute. We are waiting
for the guns.

THE CHINESE WRITERS VISIT NOTRE DAME

i.

"Gambay," they teach me
and I raise the wine, the sun-
red glass to Wu Qaing, author of
Raise High the Small Shiny Carbine
and Li Ying, *Red Willow* poet
of the coastal front. Outside,
the band is marching; autumn splays
its gold about the lawns.

We raise the glass again,
feast on smiles. I try
to tell them I have never been
to *the mountain of red flowers*,
to *the quiet sentry post*. They nod,
do not understand. The interpreter asks:
What is the subject of my poems?

ii.

At lunch, Zhang Jie, the only woman,
pulls me to her chair. Her critics
find too much love theme in *Weighted Wings*,
too much gloom.

We tell each other titles, towns,
methods of work, but our subject
is the same: how windows frame
the allotted light, sadness floats
with the leaf in the pool. We know
what women know.

Time to leave, and she takes my hand,
fumbles a camera from her purse.
She pulls me toward the stairs,
and we run into sunlight, into frisbeed
lawns, into *shadowless grass leaf*,
the arrow of noon.

iii.

When reed catkins turn white
somewhere in Peking, a woman
will pause at a basket of photographs.
She will take a plum from the table,
caress it. *Under reddening sky*,
she will translate my eyes,
the lines of my smile.

In Umbria

for Katherine

i.

Like any travelers,
we have packed the past—
old loves, old failures—
a wardrobe of mismatched bondings.

It's the curse of Eve,
you tell me: "All your longing
shall be for the man,
and he shall lord it over you." Well,
we are past the age of being lorded now,
though the longing may not cease.

ii.

The dust that man was created from
is yellow here. Women sit in doorways
making vessels of their own: a water jug,
a dragon plate, a bowl to snatch the light
from streets of soft pink stone. Up at dawn,
I see a muzzled dog, a clutch of vine,
street sweepers crooked as their brooms.
Even here all streets twist down to memory,
and memory twists back to earth.

iii.

You join me in the cypress trees,
the path of ancient saints,
show me how they climb the air,
their separate shadows each to each—
how they leave the cleanest line of shade.
We share chocolate from Perugia,
a sweetness made from bitter fruit,
watch a hawk's slow landing.
The dust on our ankles is a blessing of sorts.
We take the yellow road to Damiano.

iv.

A late sun throws ribs of light
across Assisi's square. We stand
at the fountain but do not throw coins.
The air lifts up, its own sweet slip
of current, and we are here, alive,
in Umbria, and well. The photographs
will show sun across our shoulders,
a light that warms without demanding,
a space that holds but does not grip.

GETTING THROUGH SUNDAYS

for Arthur Oberg

The ghosts of Sunday are small.
Even as a child you felt the gap
in the afternoon, the restlessness
you could not exorcise, tipping dominos
in your grandmother's house, the men
snoring in their chairs, the women smiling
like sisters-in-law. It was a space
too pale to be labeled grief, a concave fret
of something missed, as though
you knew in advance the lovers
you'd lose, the clocks that would tick
long past their last winding. Once

in a high coastal town, the future
beckoning across the bright water,
you waited through Sunday anesthetized,
while up in the turret, a window dropped,
trapped a hundred butterflies
who died there in the sun.
The next day was dark.
You swept frail and folded corpses in a dustpan,
threw splinters of flight to the wind.

Now you listen to the radio,
to rain that falls on all of Indiana.
You pick dead leaves from your plants,
think of all the letters you owe,

and how strange you feel—as though
some hollow behind your eyes
were suddenly enclosed—as though
under your skin, vaporous wings
stirred, stuttered awake, and rose.

LETTER TO AN INSOMNIAC

Suppose you took a different street
the day of the accident. Suppose
you fell through water
instead of glass, your ribs
folding like petals, the air
unruptured, the day intact.

Suppose you let the phone ring
one rainy night, the door wide open.
The man you jilted last year returns.
Suppose his fingers have sharpened;
suppose a knife in his voice.

Suppose you took that plane
from Chicago—the DC-10
that flew straight into news.
Or suppose, in the airport,
you sit next to a stranger
with frost-bitten eyes. Suppose
he kisses you, offers you marriage
or money, a job on the pipeline.
Suppose you packed nothing
you'd care to bring back.

Suppose you do not read this.
Suppose you never admit
what your waking denies:
all choices are final
but only one is your last.

Think of yourself on a train
going westward, the tracks
suturing up your past. Night
flows over like water; the window
gives you nothing back; the berth
is coffin-sized . . .

It is not what you think.
It is Nebraska or North Dakota,
nothing darker. Suppose
you believe me. Morning
will come, stations spring up
in the thistles. Suppose you sleep.
The line will continue.
The conductor will wake you
before the last stop.

. . . family history

FAMILY HISTORY

My mother will not say "the pigs
ate out the bricks" in those years
so lean there was no turnip blood
and cold snouts sucked a clay foundation.

Old aunts scowl through her prose,
and she writes: "The house
had to be abandoned; bricks crumbled . . ."

She lists dates, years, siblings
tumbled like a wagonload of beets
(though she does not say it)
out of muffled darkness, small
disturbances in sleep. She writes
a clean and tidy record.

My mother does not say she stood
as I see her, slim girl on the plains
of too much sorrow—the crumbled house,
the hatchery gone, the father's death
rounding her mouth like a stone

—does not say she left that graying house
while a spotted sow, her teats gone slack,
her nostrils dusty, moved toward a foundation
I see clearly now, sniffing out
the blood of a house, rooting, rooting . . .

Rites of Women

i.

One turns the whetstone,
one holds the blade.
When the edge is ground
from the April noon,
they move to the cellar
through flat, cyclone doors,
my mother, my grandmother,
low amid the gunnysacks.

Potatoes fall
in their laps, an eye
for each chunk, a quick blade
into moist white flesh, the snap
of the knife. Trying to learn,
I snap the sprouts that thrust their way
through the gunnysacks, white, swollen,
big as my five-year-old thumb.
"Child! Stop that!" my grandmother says.
"What can you be thinking of?
This is how things grow!"

ii.

Steam rises from guts as my breath
rises winter mornings when I wake
to frosted windows, a furnace burned low.
"Casings," my grandmother calls them,

and they spill on the oilcloth,
casks of blue and steaming pearls
fetched like a dowry in dishpans
from the bellowing walls of the shed.

I stroke the opalescent loops, poke
membrane like the skin on open cream.
"Next year," I say,
"I will watch when they do it."
"No you won't," my mother says.

To kill the steer is a rite of men.

iii.

In the time of thinning cabbages,
I stoop with my mother to the waving row,
try to take the discards from her,
hoard them for some garden of my own.
"There is room for so much—no more,"
she says, and limp stems go
to the compost heap. No grief
among the cabbages, no tears
for what must go. She leans
on the rake, looks down at me:
"It's like pruning," she says,

and I know the rest: it's the ritual
of choosing—it's how we live.

LITTLE SISTERS

This birthday I have reached the age
where my mother bore
the last of her dead daughters—
one that was whisked away
before its first clean cry
could scour the naked room, the later two
a blue that refused to brighten.

"Baby Girl, Infant Daughter of . . ."
the little markers said,
and I listened from behind the stove
in her last pregnancy,
watched her body swell and sag,
knew from the shape
of those whispered words
that something was amiss—
she was weighted already
with two small stones.

Summer mornings I called them forth—
the little sisters I had never seen—
made them faces
from the old ache
in the air above the garden,
hair like mine
from the grassy space
where root crops should have been.

I learned of blood tests, transfusions,
a factor called Rh,
my little sisters
dreaming their aquatic days
on lethal ropes, my mother
almost dead.

Now at the kitchen table
lighting candles on a cake,
I am empty-handed,
empty-wombed,
no daughters to give her
as she counts again
my miraculous birth,
fourth and forceps-born,
her last survivor in that war
of blood with family blood.

I reach for her hand and hold it,
but there are spaces here,
tender lacunae we cannot fold away.
Still somewhere the hand-stitched garments,
the gingham quilts, the counting game.
Still the soot-smudged corner
where I crouched beneath the stovepipe
and fingered like a rosary
the small pebbles of their names.

DUST

The sky was a plate of curds
the autumn Uncle Reuben came, three days late,
in the afternoon mail. His mortal whey
gone to thin smoke above a southern town,
he came north stamped, insured,
delivered RFD to the roadside box
where my mother waited. Nothing
inside but a plastic bag, she said,
and closed it. Kept him
in the cool front room
till prairie skies glazed blue,
a plate washed clean and empty,
and the priest could come.

My parents refused
to distribute the ash—
they will nothing to scatter—
the posthole digger drew a tidy plug,
a sweet core of grassland,
and they dropped him in.

Augering into another autumn,
I remember his smile, his scars from the fire
at the dry cleaning plant. I put down
tulips between the hard frosts,
crocus bulbs with absurd little navels . . .

And so the story ends: no flesh to decay,
no bones to toss up centuries later—
only a woman with a trowel in hand,
only this wind
across the edge of Indiana, this swift
and gritty eddy of leaves,
a scent, perhaps, of something relinquished,
sand in the mouth,
a speck in the eye.

THE NEW APPLIANCES

First there was the stove
the year his heart went bad,
a new Maytag after the Monarch range
simmered thirty years off their electric bill.
Then the Christmas we all could sense
something was amiss: a gassy smell,
a scent like danger, perhaps like death,
worn-out valves no longer pumping warmth
through rooms where she stokes him daily
with low-salt food like the doctor said.

After the new furnace, the microwave:
meals in a flash, she says,
plenty of time to count the pills
in the minutes that his oatmeal cooks.
Then, last month, the stroke.

It was hardly anything, she says:
a brief ungluing of eyes,
words that stuck, food that tumbled
from the left side of his mouth.
He is well enough to go to town
when they choose the new wash machine,
automatic, a real time-saver,
no more rinse tubs, no cellar steps to climb,
no more wringers for his old gray socks,
fibers thinning beneath her very hand.

It's the new pipes from the wellhouse
make all the difference, she says,
—as though years were a cistern
she could bypass when dry—
And you should get yourself a freezer, she says,
and try those herbed salt-substitutes.
Such good flavor, she says,
like spring coming right out of the garden again,
like water when we could drink it
straight from the well.

. . . the many kinds of doubt

The Many Kinds of Doubt

i.

First, there was the river.
Dark July, and you led me down.

Fish-flies littered the streets about us,
dove at our feet in their eagerness to die.
In my childhood town, they bulldozed
them from the bridges, slippery death
drifting like the empty hulls of snow.

Here you took my hand,
moved from the shadow of the bridge
to the shadow of the pilings.

It's safe, you said. Come down.

ii.

We waited out Christmas
the year we couldn't leave; windchill
a minus 87, and every pipe
its own icy wreath. At dinner
in the only restaurant open, we burned
the brief fuel of what there was to say. Did you
have turkey as a child? Did your children
like their gifts? Does adultery
give the injured one an unquestioned right to leave?

43

No one was going anywhere. We split
the bill and left. How often
do vagaries of weather
immobilize the heart?

iii.

I would be a better Christian
(you say) if I'd leave the saving
to someone else. Like these nights
we hear traffic behind the plaster,
the spill of something crumbling overhead.
Squirrels in the attic, you say,
and go off to sleep, but it's more than that:
something scrapes and gnaws
the wires that used to connect.

This is the difference between us:
when trouble comes,
one of us sleeps and one of us wakes,
one of us rests and one of us rises,
tapping the walls in a white flannel gown,
listening at corners, testing the sockets
that have started to spark.

One of us dreams and one of us watches,
knowing what the dreamer fears:
that some night the other will descend the stair,
begin to strip paper from the living room,
dismantle the lights, pull out
the bricks one by one
with her own hands, until she finds
the beast in the wall, until she has torn
the whole house down.

THINGS COME IN FROM THE COLD

These shortened days
I wake to cold, to wasps like snow
against the window where they whine
a frantic nest into the eaves.

Things come in from the cold
in autumn. Crickets comment on my sleep.
They have claimed the cellar,
the coal-bin; the field mice

have claimed last season's shoe.
One clear morning, wings break
inside the chimney—something falls.
You tell your son:

in autumn things fulfill themselves.
"You mean they die," he says,
and there it is again: that field
of goldenrod bending, the lines

you trace on my palm, that spider
dropping from a single thread. You take my hand
although we have no hope
the seasons will stop spinning—

that leaves will cling, green and wet,
or the old worm turn more slowly.
"—But come in," you say,
and for a time, however brief,

winter is only a softer light,
and across the ice, we see distance glowing.

46

PLAYING THE BELLS

Five stories up, we climb the steeple to play
this carillon against the dusk, against the rain
that returns us to darkness as surely as to day.

In a tar-papered room, you sit and sway
above levers like spools, like a loom ordained
to music. Five stories up, where we climbed to play

these spindles of sound, I poke through the splay
of dust: droppings, bottles, dead pigeon remains—
a presage of darkness as surely as of day.

Then "Alouette" rings above the hymnal's gray
tones, your sudden whimsy, and I strain—
five stories up, in the steeple where you play—

to hold it longer, to keep this bright foray
against October's dying, against the twilight pain
that turns us toward darkness more surely than toward
day.

Notes ending, I will the resonance to stay—
to be stronger than twilight, stronger than rain,
five stories up in the steeple where we play
against the turn of darkness, believing surely in the day.

GEESE CROSSING THE ROAD

Winter again,
and the heart chokes down a little,
driving mid-country, the windshield
an esplanade of rain.

Past prairie towns
scattered on the soil like ancient vertebrae,
I slow the car for a farmer's geese,
a haughty promenade, not to be hurried
as they step out their scorn
of rain, each feather in place,
feet glowing like a beacon.

In another town, you are less secure
than they, wearing my troubled love
like an ill-stitched coat
against such rudiments of weather.

Dear heart,
whatever grief I've caused you,
the truth is this: love at midlife
is not flight, not
buoyant migration to another plane,
but small journeys, sudden
new species of touch, a proud arc
in the lifting neck, a stay
against depletion. It is these geese
crossing the road, calling us back
to some primordial attention
we had wandered from, some forgotten state
where we too touched the earth
and stepped out the essence
of whiteness, of sureness, of morning.

Ice Climber

(Lake Michigan, March)

I have followed you into a land
not land but frozen as a dream
might freeze the last wakes of longing
or a photograph might still the cliffs
of storm from breaking on the beach.

You point to fault lines, cleavage,
the face of an ice-cliff about to break,
but I follow in your steps
climbing the pock-marked waves,
slipping down an icy swell
thirty feet above a concave sea.

Below us, waves create new caverns,
ice floes bounce like flagstones afloat.
"We are walking on the moon," I say.
"No," you say. "We walk a tideless sea."

You tell me again of danger:
what is shining will not stay.
But we are standing in sunlight,
the ice floes rustle like leaves.
A breeze touches my hair as you
might touch, as though time too
could solidify, and seasons from now
we could still be here,
riding this crest to the sea.

FREIGHT

You say the trains are your fear of death
hurling blindly from corners
across the tunnel you must walk,
your luggage lost,
through the underground of dreams.

We are both of us weighted,
our lives crisscrossed
with former destinations,
the tickets we have never used.

Your son can name them: *Santa Fe reefer,*
F-7 engine, bay-window caboose . . .
He builds tracks through your house
with his rolling stock. The past
is forever steaming through.

My ploy is swerving: I dodge crossings,
rear like a mare when the gate goes down,
fear couplings that might pull me again
down a track I didn't choose.

Then, why do we return nightly—
you to the tunnels, I to the boxcar roof
where dirty and frightened, my clothing torn,
I cling like a miser to the speeding steel?

What is it I rush to, my belly inching
from car to car, as though no gauge
were ever fast enough, no station
ever sufficiently near? Why
the flowing river on my right,
the row of lamps? Why in my mouth
this secret glee, humming faster than the fear?

The Moment of Loss Is Always Familiar

The moment of loss is always familiar:
it is the first breath drawn
outside the hospital room, the dull
menstrual ache of expulsion, the step
you miss down a stairway of rain,
the letter you find months later.

It's the moment you wake
and know something's wrong: the crib
is empty, the windshield's cracked,
the lining ripped out of everything.
It's the miscarried winter when ice
breaks the eaves, when you dream

you are back in that field,
the cattle astray, the farm lights receding.
Owls are swifter than soft, pulsing fur,
and you run, run through the heart of the corn,
each tassel exploding, each leaf
a sharp-tongued sneer: Who? How long?

Loss is the moment you stand still
in that field, the wind dropped,
the cattle gone. Sound, like a heartbeat,
has ceased, and you are the space
the wind has removed, you are
the loss, the one no one is seeking.

After It Ended

I slept and dreamed of Ireland,
cottages wearing whitewash
like a flag of truce, cycles
rolling at leisure through the lanes.

There was no stress in that simple life:
old carts, wheels throbbing like a heart,
carried fresh cream to the gate;
light from the sea came washing by,
a silky weight upon the window frame.

But then I woke.
I stepped from that dream,
as a skier steps without the skis,
a skater on land, a man in a cast
who must learn again to put one foot down
and then another, making a path
through uncertainty.

If it has really ended,
Ireland is stones, a toppled stile
in the oldest hedge,
a bare, ruined choir,
where late you sang, and now lie down.
It is your longest bones
settling for a single slab
no matter where or with whom
you are sleeping.

BIRDS THAT DO NOT FLY

are creatures of the plain,
the savannah, the middling plateaus
where things have a habit of bogging down.
Why they chose the earth
is a mystery—chose symmetrical plumes,
flat breastbones, over the eagle's prow.
It takes a certain slant
to bend the air.

Perhaps they were preoccupied:
food to catch and both feet on the ground.
Or perhaps, like a woman waking
from an endless affair, they were not sure
what clue they missed, what somnolence
came over them
while everything else was taking off.

Sometimes at dawn
I number them: ostrich, emu,
the dodo of Mauritius,
their great toes dug in,
their feathers tender as a chick's.
Like them, I lift my neck
beneath a sky spread out like a testament,
scanning only to scan again
what flickers and glints
and is gone.

WHAT IF A WOMAN

forty-three years old and
driving her car down the street
just after the lover
who accused her of terrible things
had found another girl
and sunlight was scaling
the tavern roofs
and spring stood in the trees
a silk-winged Icarus
ready to leap
and she whispered to herself
"I am alone
alone
and I will not tell
how lovely it is
I will not tell
anyone at all"
and she floated right up
through the roof of the car
right into the folds
of the silk-winged sky
above a dozen maple trees
unleafed as yet
who leaned back to watch
and applauded?

. . . different stars

(a New Zealand journal)

MIDAIR

If asked
I could list
three reasons for migration:
    to look ahead
    to leave behind
    to try to keep up
    with the earth's vicious spin

I packed for the latter
—for new names to call
the gaps in the sky.

Aotearoa, the Maoris call New Zealand—
land of the long white cloud—

From the seat of this DC-10
I see no clouds, only
the shirred splendor of water.
A clean slate, I say to myself,
an ocean of erasure . . .

The man next to me
stirs in his seat,
buries himself in his copy of *Time*.

Another reason
I could add to the list:
in the dark we crossed the dateline.
I am a day ahead of my past.

Different Stars

I am learning the meaning of *antipodes*,
the opposite, the polar star,
a day gone from life
as the plane skims the date line
then all direction gone.

It's not the left-hand driving,
not the telephone dial I turn from below.
Cold blows up from the south here;
water goes down the drain hole
the other way round.
In May's quickening dusks,
time is the truest vertigo,
June a bright winter
where yellow leaves fall past camellia buds
and cabbage trees
fake their way into being palms.

I can fake nothing,
not a knowledge of streets,
not a knowledge of stars
these cold June nights
I stand beneath a sky turned round,
the hunter askew,
the bear herself
all out of joint . . .

Across the Tasman Sea,
the Northern Crown
becomes a boomerang—

a lofty throw
from the Dreaming Time.
Here the Milky Way,
that basket of stars,
that long white shark,
is Tane's net staked out
on Rangi's cloak—
old Father-Sky
whose dark embrace
once covered Mother-Earth
with night.

We become what we believe,
the stories we tell
to make the random right.
It is the reason for war,
for failures at love,
for all that occurs
under different stars,
each of us
our own coordinates,
sure of our latitudes,
sure that this time
the ball's in the net,
the arrow's slung,
the one right tale
that will speak our lives
is here and has begun.

MOUNT MANGANUI

Like other mountains
he was allowed to walk
each night when Father-Sky
secured the darkness with his cloak;
and walk he did
until the night he found his love,
fairest of the Kaimai Range,
tucking her own soft peaks
into another's crevasses.

Then he turned to the sea,
to Hine-moana, old ocean
of rage, the only place
in which to drown himself.

The rest of the story is sadder:
Perhaps he was held back by fear,
a bad knee, shin-splints
from all that walking . . .
Perhaps he paused,
devising a way to make her feel the worst.
At any rate, he loitered.

And there he is now,
at the harbor's edge,
where Dawn, the swift tattler,
caught him—up to his knees
in the drink, his belly
broad as day, his shoulders hunched
against what every lover ought to know:
the uselessness of all such gestures.

A LEGEND

In the Dreaming Time,
kangaroo men and wallaby men
had faces that carved themselves
on the face of the Rock:
skull, brain, the spilled boulder-guts
of the man who searched and searched
for the elusive sign—
    the rabbit-legged cloud,
    the shape of the snake—
his dream a long migration
over red, red sand
beneath the low acacia trees
his guts bursting at last—
a swift canyon of despair,
a rocky tumble into dream time.

To remember is the same
as to dream, the old guide says—
to be in that place
which is not here,
cannot be seen or touched,
yesterday as invisible,
as remote as last night's stars,
the past a flicker
on the same screen as sleep.

I could tell another legend:
there is a woman I know
who dreamed three love affairs:
    a November lake
    a runner in sand
    whales diving in a northern sea.
She too is searching.
What she has not learned
are the facts of history—
that the migration of love
cannot enter another's dreaming time,
cannot always explain
those tracks on the face
of the old, old moon,
the meaning of boulders.

PHOTOGRAPHS: NORTH ISLAND

I. Lake Waikaremoana

The children of Tane
hid in these woods —
light-skinned, red-haired,
naked as their flutes —
or so the legend says.

I believe it.
Light is different here
deep in the bush.
Refracted on the polar ice,
it splinters on the lake,
makes a harlequin of shade.

I do not tell you this,
but bits of me elude the air,
dance behind the rimu trees.

II. Pirongia

Maidens seeking fernroot
took this path,
silver fronds brushing against them,
fingers of mist trailing their hair.
And some of them heard spectral flutes —
the koauau or putorino —

luring them up, up
to the summit of fog,
the mossy beds of giants
who were not men,
who could pipe away their wills,
enthrall them with music forever.

At the top of the trail
we find a goat skull stuck
in a small dead tree,
a clearing stripped of fern.
Those who slept with giants
never returned, you tell me.

We laugh, begin our descent
to the bellbird's song.
Then lichen on the trees,
clinging like hoarfrost.
Here and everywhere:
small, skeletal desires.

III. Rangitaiki River

Rapids, rocks,
water lacing the air.
In the photo, we've been pitched
to the bottom of the raft.

I will remember the quiet stretch:
the flight of the fan-tail
beside us. The wood pigeon
perched and at rest.

IV. Cape Reinga

for Kate and Lin

This is the last
of the ends of the earth,
land's finger pointing straight
to the departure place, straight
to the old pohutakawa tree
where the *wairua* leaped—
stripped spirits of the dead—
when the seas collided
and bull-kelp surged aside,
and water was the last,
the most sacred entrance.

It is said the *wairua*
tied flax leaves in knots,
plaiting their long journey north,
rustled unseen through toi-toi
and bracken, the warriors in platoons
when the battle was lost, women
leaving nikau leaves, treeferns,
ghostly obsidian tokens.

We stand at the border
of force with force, sea
with sea, the blue Pacific
abutting the greener Tasman.
On the last slope
below the lighthouse drop,
we pose without fear
against the edge of the sky.
We are friends. We have crossed
what we needed to cross.
The flax is green, the air
untangled, the sunlight arrives
and arrives . . .

WELLINGTON

for Varvara

This July, this winter
of reversed perceptions,
we flew south into a storm so mean
the plane shuddered like a bumblebee
across the bay. Two were already dead
below us—the police launch
splitting like an oyster
when the storm slit its shell,
the road past Seatoun closed.

It was a week of closures:
the play we braved Chinatown
to see, the cable car, the dark
coming down like a fist.
At lunch on Lambton Quay,
I told you of the man I left,
my face coming clear
in the mirror again,
the eyes of insomnia
shut. That night
the phone rang an ending
in our hotel: your husband's voice
connected somewhere else.
This is a windy bit
I have to row, you said.
We closed the drapes
against the ripping sound.

The Last Time I Entered Grief

it was a country
less populous than this,
and only five were residents:

a girl in a thin chemise,
bending too low
on the riverbank,
her hair turning to leaves,
her wrists
becoming skin on the water

a sailor arriving too late,
his watch cap pulled low,
his duffle bag tight,
something ticking like a clock
every step of the docks
he must walk to get to Tauranga

an old woman, of course,
a new shearing at her feet,
her body a bobbin the color of blood,
her mornings pulled each by each
from the dark and spinning wheel

a boy I didn't expect,
chucking his clothes
in the clump of wild flax,
racing down the black sand beach,
wanting to yell:
well, thank God, that's over

and somewhere in the streets
of a town much like Dunedin,
a dog, a mongrel bitch
who does not know
she is separate from these,
does not understand
that trees and grass are anything but self,
that sky is not her farthest glance
from which a vast, inchoate part
is missing

Tarawera: The Lost Terraces

*on the 100th anniversary of the
mountain's eruption*

i.

If the phantom war canoe
sails again these waters,
sails again through the monster's breath
as when Tuhotoariki
released him from this mountain,
will the Terraces arise, pink and white,
from their lava depths, that eighth
wonder of the world, a mountainside
of lovers' pools, silica petals,
water spilling over lily lips
until the mountain pitched them down,
like a swift igniting of flowers?

ii.

If I ride the dark water
to these steaming cliffs
where black swans dive
beneath a mountain's scars,
will I weight my losses
like a fishing line, toss out
again and again until something snags

(in strange countries, which is greater—
the loss of what you've known
or the loss of what you've not?)

iii.

If the *tohunga* speaks,
old Maori priest,
chanting in a sulfurous wind,
will these words be heard or lost?

Before the columns of fire,
before the chunks of sky rained down,
there was the battle, the serpent,
the old-old time, love
with all that it generates. Love.
Love with what it consumes.

PHOTOGRAPHS: SOUTH ISLAND

for Avis, my niece

I. Otago Peninsula

Remember this
about that secret bay:

the paddock cliffs,
the hoof-wide trail, penguins
homing in the evening light,
their clown-shoe route
across the slanted sun . . .

And this: the one who stood
sentry on the rocks,
luring us away from nests,
from home, from lupins
flowing like the valley's veil,
to an absence of sound,
of speech, an absence of all
but the way we drew breath,
the penguin on the edge
of nothing but itself,
rocks remaining rocks,
the sea, the sea.

II. Franz Joseph Glacier: the Terminal Moraine

This is a place for the middle-aged—
the signposts marking year by year
the glacier's retreat, the past
a long scar of splintered rock.

And you, dear heart, are young,
your bandana more flagrant
than the Danger sign
as you climb up and up
to the avalanche zone.

What would I tell you
if I could call from this ridge?
Not: "Stay!" Not: "Be frightened!"
But that trees are reclaiming
this cicatrix of rock, lichen
softening the cuts, vines binding up.
From where I sit, waiting in rain,
nothing despairs here,
nothing denies.

III. St. Kilda Coast

Women on their own
wake like this, wind rocking
a beach motel, the rain chanting
alone, alone . . .

Our cameras packed,
we focus voices across the dark,
across the strangeness
of related lives, naming towns,
parents, the secrets we kept
from the family hearth, old
storms that now invade the room . . .

A tremor of nerves
I say of the wind,
a former lover's moan . . .

No, you say—a tympany.
The orchestra trips you took
too young. The vibraphone.

ANOTHER JOURNAL: NEW ZEALAND, 1895

This is a history of spaces,
not wars, not farms
ripped like green transgressions from these hills.
This is about needles lost in floorboards
and griddles made from broken saws,
about the way
he felt for something in my skirts
on the voyage over, my father already dead,
my sister swept to sea
in an illness like a storm.

              "This land
is ours," he wrote that winter
of berries, fern roots ("eat
what the Maoris eat"), green kea parrots,
their underwings already bled
with colors of the womb. I did the dutiful:
potatoes and parsnips, stones
for my own hearth when we moved
from the *whare*, the fern hut
whose shadows were my bridal lace.

His ledgers are on the shelf:
wages, crops, a visit from an Auckland judge,
the price of cemetary plots. I stitched
another story in a quilt: the shape
of tiny fish-mouths on my nipples
when the pain was done, the pleasured swirl
of the element we swam in; round "o's"
for the "ought" of an egg, for spaces

underground where steam vents forth,
where glowworms cast
their fishing nets; ovals
for the sounds of these new names:
Oamaru. Te Awamutu. Rotorua . . .

At sixty-eight I learned to write.

What does it mean
to make a mark on the ledger's page,
to tell as men tell, fixing forever
the color of uncertain skies?

Some pages I leave empty.
Some pages for the times I stood
at the kitchen window
or the bottom paddock pool,
not touching anything,
feeling myself a vacancy
not even clouds could fill.
Sometimes I wonder
what colors would explode
if I were to rise a little from the earth
and could push back the air,
could move myself into the space
between my body and the sky?

WAITOMO: THE RIVER UNDER THE EARTH

When we had descended far enough
I remembered it all:
    How it is dark
    when you enter the boat
    how the others are strangers
    how the ferryman is silent
    having warned in some upper passage
    that the current will be swift.

I said nothing
as he poled us through the water,
though some among us murmured,
some among us turned.
What good was there in speaking?
—Everyone I loved
was in another country,
everything I owned
was locked away and far.

I watched those we had left grow smaller,
black shapes on a black and weary shore.
This is Lethe, I said,
but I meant Styx. I meant Charon
and all those old stories,
all those crossings
that can never be recrossed.

When darkness was thicker than the water,
I remembered the rest.
I dropped the little I was holding,
turned my face upward as we had been told.
Glowworms clustered somewhere above us—
a newly constellated heaven
of blue and equal stars—
and long before the passage widened,
I knew the rhythm of the river,
long before the light came,
I was ready to float free.